CLAY VESSELS

AND OTHER POEMS

POETRY
JOHN McNAMEE

WOODCUTS
ROBERT F. McGOVERN

SHEED & WARD
Kansas City

Sheed & Ward™ is a service of The National Catholic Reporter Publishing Company.

───────────────────◆───────────────────

Library of Congress Cataloguing-in-Publication Data

McNamee, John P., 1933-
    Clay vessels and other poems : poetry / John McNamee ; woodcuts, Robert F. McGovern.
        p.   cm.
    ISBN: 1-55612-812-6 (pbk. : alk. paper)
    1. Christian poetry, American.   I. Title.
PS3563.C388364C58   1995
811'.54--dc20   95-30251
                                                                          CIP

───────────────────◆───────────────────

Published by: Sheed & Ward
                    115 E. Armour Blvd.
                    P.O. Box 419492
                    Kansas City, MO 64141-6492

To order, call: (800) 333-7373

Cover design by James F. Brisson.

Poems

Introduction vii

Clay Vessels 2

Advent 3

Haitian House Guest 4

Easter Longing 5

Footwashing 6

A Day Away 7

Inclusion as a Form of Gratitude 9

Writing 12

Love Light 19

Madonna 20

Requiem for a Sister 21

Hospital 22

Spring 23

Holy Thursday: Mandatum 29

Good Friday: Adoration of the Cross 30

Holy Saturday: the Great Vigil 31

Easter 32

In Memoriam: Franz Jäggerstätter 35

In Memoriam: Simone Weil 43

A Gloss on the Obituaries: Graham Greene 1904–1991 45

Sandymount 46

Inishowen Head 47

Retreat Hospitality (for Loman, O.F.M.) 48

Oratory: Easter Friday 49

Traffic Light 50

France: Inflight 55

Paris: Église Saint-Séverin 57

Paris: Église d'Auteuil 58

Greece: Cape Sunion Temple of Poseidon 59

Munich: Frauenplatz 62

New Mexico 63

Bavaria: Ettal Monastery 64

City Church 65

Woodcuts

Artist at Work   viii

Poet in Cavernous Space   x

Such as a Rose   1

By the Gate of the Sacred (Gerard Manley Hopkins)   8

City at Evening   13

Fall Leaves   14

Urban Youth in a Tree of Dreams   15

Urban Boy as Thinker   16

Moaning Buildings   17

Mother, Child and the Dawn   18

Dark Forest   24

Behold the Man   25

Crucifixion   26

Crucifixion in Light   27

Crown of Thorns   28

Alleluia   33

Door to the Path Taken   34

Franziska in the Shadow   36

Franz Illumined   39

Go with God   40

The Distant Water, the Trees and Church   41

I Wondered Anxiously (Simone Weil)   42

Where there is Life there is not Peace (Graham Greene)   44

Irish Fate   51

Music and Song the Light and Fire of Education   52

Folk Singer   53

Bird with Round Wing   54

Sun Over the Loch   56

Pilgrim of the Mountain   60-61

Rose Cosmos   66

Introduction

It was McGovern who first spoke to me about his sense that we had within us the power or the chance, maybe the need, to make of something ordinary, something sacred. This notion has a history old enough that he used the Latin phrase, "consecratio mundi," the world consecrated, the potential to create, to make something out of nothing or not much, to shape harmonies from the noise all about.

The images and poems here were made by two friends. One a woodcarver, husband, father and now even grandfather, professor of art, historian, rooted solid as the maple at the doorstep of his home. The other a priest, restless contemplative; stuck, stationed, posting himself in the "projects of the poor" for a lifetime. Some common origins: their surnames speak of ancestry, births timed to the Depression and that humbling of American spirit, boyhoods on the streets and in the row houses of immigrants' West Philadelphia. Their growing years tuned to the sounds and sadnesses of a world elsewhere at war. Then different paths to different stations.

McNamee is a man alone, though nearly every waking hour he is surrounded by others: both at his beck and call – the secretary, the housekeeper, the parish minister – and those he serves; always the doorbell, the phone ringing, the letter asking attention to passages in families not his own, tending births and christenings, the growing up and graduations, and weddings, the visits to the sick, the jailed, the dying. He always consoling, comforting, challenging and encouraging – with it all always marked by an aloneness, prayer in an empty church, the nightly ascent to a bed alone. He has a sense of paths not taken, of the promise of self made to a church that seems too often to have become a backwater of foolish men in medieval costume, curators of a museum that has collected stuff of no interest to anyone anymore.

McGovern on the other hand, a man engaged, bound, social. As much as he shapes wood with gouge he is shaped by the kids and students and colleagues and friends. Yet, with him also, so many hours alone – hours with hammer, gouge, chisel, his imagination, and the wood. McGovern, as contemporary of Jonas Salk, knows of the achievements of this century and the irreversibility of fate. As deeply as McNamee's poems evoke a sense of other paths, other decisions, McGovern's works recognize the impossibility of a destiny other than one's own – the knife cuts once.

There is in both a lingering matter they see as faith. There is in both an undimmed capacity to wait for something sacred to erupt into a profane and broken world. Their words and woodcuts are their squinting, their pointed fingers.

Cuts

The woodcuts copied by high speed press for this book begin with a surfaced slab of wood; basswood often, sometimes cherry, pine or boxwood. McGovern goes at the wood with a gouge. Each cut into wood becomes light on these pages. Wood left alone presents ink to the press of the paper: black. McGovern works in the light. Start there to see his images.

He buttons this book together with two roses; frontispiece and end piece. Both full blossom. The front one in two dimensions, the only light let in is the line of gouge, with the crossing grain of wood hinting at a receding plane beyond a transparent flower. The rose at back curvaceous, suggesting another dimension, most wood cut away and the darkness the woodcutter left are the recesses of the petals. Straightforward enough. McGovern is no trickster but I must, if I am to see what he wants to show, pay attention to the dark and the cut before the suggestion of light and shadow takes me to the representation of a rose.

There is a sad Christ image, "Behold the Man" (Pilate's demand), printed opposite "Dark Forest." The one easy for the eye to understand is the mysterious one. The other, the abstraction, the image is actually

more direct – tangled woods in half-light with half-seen shapes. McGovern gives me the tangle of the woods and then lets me rest easier with the Christ. Note the strike of knife in the shaping of Christ's torso, no different than the shape of lights and darks on opposite page.

Those representations – people, scapes, scenes and still things – are only part of his work. McGovern gouges light onto page when he cuts away wood.

Sounds

Early monks sang the words of divine scripture. They took the scriptures as script or score, not text; the sound of God on their lips, in their ears, not correspondence from one absent the scene. Hard for us literate people to distinguish the word from its grapheme. Read McNamee's poems like the monks sang scripture, not the way we read the morning paper. It is in the sounds.

His lines go in breath spaces. Breaths go between each line to set the rhythm. He suggests some other silences in his laying the poem on the page;

"beside us   clay cups"

is to take longer to say than

"beside us clay cups."

"...clay cups..." is the next image, not the completion of the previous one.

There are other silences in the poems that will be missed if read as text. The sound of "...grim ghost ships at concrete anchor" with all eleven plosive consonants rocking the breath's soundwaves back and forth between lips, palate, tongue and larynx, are real waves of energy bouncing against the impediments of our voicing, buffeting our insides. The sound is the sense. McNamee lofts gentled sounds to evoke, re-present to the reader, the small grace illumined by the ghetto woman living in a desolate space.

Just as there are staccato rhythms in the length and depth of McGovern's gouges into the wood, so in McNamee's lines, there are sonorities and silences that guide toward the small earthy graces that have been given to these men.

Sense

There is a materiality, a carnality in these works that is no element of style but is the substance of them: sounds of the words, and light-strikes of the images, reflections of light bouncing from the pages into our eyes. McNamee and McGovern are sensing the way into a presence in the world, a new approach to faith and spirituality that does not avoid

embracing creation in its messy and confusing wholeness. The people living about the Eastern Mediterranean a few thousand years ago came to a great assertion: "The world makes sense." The Greek word "logos" refers to this. The act of creation was to form this harmony, this logos, from the chaos.

Four images by McGovern, as many lines by McNamee as in all the other poems combined, center this volume. The images and the poem were separately made by McNamee and McGovern after a journey they had made together. They had gone to Austria to the home of Franziska Jägerstätter, widow of Franz Jägerstätter, a father of three daughters, thirty-six years old when killed as a resister of the Nazi warmakers in 1943. To most of us this Franz fellow was an unnecessary hero, a headstrong fool, maybe even a man of disturbed thought in a world that had gone stark mad. To McGovern and McNamee something else was going on in this man's life, this woman's life – one partnered life really – worth the pilgrimage. How they see so differently this coming/going on of something sacred in an ordinary country family:

> A neighbor out early saw him leaving
> looking back that February morning
> toward this farmhouse from the gravel path
> framed now by this kitchen window...

Franz on his way toward inevitable death.

And McGovern's image shows it from the other side, from the interior of the home, the empty doorway through which he had departed, and path where he had gone away. The view Franziska and daughters had. The hole Franz's leaving left.

The scene is a peaceful farmhouse doorway, three children going toward church in a quiet Austrian village, in a valley out of which Franz goes, in a time of, in a place at global war, saturation bombing, mutilation, death, and vengeance never seen in the whole history of the world, not until McNamee and McGovern were boys, now looking on the scene as men at the other end of life.

McNamee asks,

> Why was Franz so alone?   Where
> the Church so woven into life?
> The Benedictine blessing of ordinary
> family   fields   and daily life?

How was it possible for there to be but one man opposing immense evil in a place so dense with the signs of faith? In McGovern's *Pilgrim of the Mountain*, the pilgrim is but a small aside in the dark swirl of mountain, rock and violent sky.

The work here of McNamee and McGovern does not assert that the world makes sense – that there is a logos. The authors do not shy from dark places, nor from reminding us that is where we often are. It is in these difficult places that they make their work. They, as in McNamee's line "...search the shadows await a late Rising...." They sense the presence of the mystery in the chaos of the world, different than predecessors who sensed the presence in the order, the harmony of the world. So toward Franz Jägerstätter they point. Here is the penetration of the sacred into the profaned: this pilgrim of the mountain.

The book has a calendar in its composition, early on an Advent wait, hopeful and expectant, and winter chill. Then the trembling wait of Lent. Easter, then Jägerstätter, the gift of a faith that demands everything in return, the ferocity of a sun that turns a lake to cloud. But also the lovely woman, her scent and shape, his pull – "Her grace graces psalms...." Earth made sacred, his desire consecrated.

And finally a rose, as at first but deeper and only a rose; then McNamee in last poem claims "sunlight pours down on darkness." We need this beauty more than bread.

Joseph P. Ferry
May, 1995

CLAY
VESSELS

AND OTHER POEMS

Clay Vessels

The last light paints the west windows
down in shadow we prepare
    the daily Birth in Bread

creatures of routine
we year round reach no farther than
    the clay vessels on the shelf
    dull as this November day

once Advent was light against the growing dark
        "Arise, Jerusalem..." etc

like everything else ritual runs out
leaving us dry as desert wadis

a stroke against this winter world
would fetch the silver back behind
    the earthenware

catch the candle flame on a shining underside
        round as the virgin's carry
whose coming feast sets her precious self
beside us   clay cups
who are also vessels

Advent

Ghetto woman
these Advent evenings
when I light wreath candles
against winter darkness
and search holy books
to feel the spirit of a season
that gathers human yearning
into hope

I remember other evenings
when the projects hovered
over Diamond Street
ghost ships at concrete anchor
and somewhere in the upper reaches
of that ruined landscape
your window wreathed in Christmas lights

taught me more of hope
than all my books and pieties

Haitian House Guest

"Christmas come early" we cry
for joy of the sudden gift
which lifts us like
becalmed sailors leaping for lines
catching new wind in slack sails
off! in salt spray and white wake

Christmas came early here
when marshals dropped you sudden
and welcome as Santa's sack

refugee   resident   alien   activist
no name suits you but
Balthasar the Wiseman

gift in hand you Creole man are creche gold
refined in suffering and separation

faith   strength   joy   flow from you
warm and gentle as your Caribbean

as in the Magi Legend
your own journey gift to us along the way

Easter Longing

Last Ash Wednesday
burying Jack Beatty in winter cold
we huddled so close around his grave that
wet sod wedged off our shoes onto his casket
making our earlier Lenten rite almost trivial.

The penitential season!
Jack's ten-month fast so awful so
wounding our faith and sense of fairness
we could only stagger to Easter leaving
the eager Lenten readings for the less exhausted.

Lent enough!
The early morning glances half prayers
half glances toward the casual coarse-grained
photo all I have of Jack against oblivion.

Morning?
Lent means March mornings more
and more wall and picture rinse orange
join a new season waking outside even
Jack in image recovers an illness-lost blush.

The eternal return.
City lots undress   embarrass
into old tires and broken glass
soon soften and grow green.

Lent-laden   death-deprived
like a sea-weary sailor looking landward
I squeeze hope from spring juice.
What I want is Easter.

Footwashing

Crouched here in half-darkness
I cup a shy heel for footwashing
my mind back in mid-March
the talk to our peace group:
The Middle East   Arab   Jew   Christian

A lenten stripping of remaining illusions
about us Peoples of the Book
whose genocidal God commands:
"Seize the land.   Take no survivors
not women, not children or even cattle."

The flawed humanity which incarnates faith
in holy wars and inquisitions can
be incandescent.   Our speaker
says that Lenten Sunday Gospel
chokes him up with

the largess required
demanded from the Older Son.
Such pulling at us
more than we measure possible.

No wonder the half-refusal
to proffer me this foot.   Reluctance
cloaked in a shudder over cold water.
Holding on I pull myself and the other
out of the bloodbath of the Tradition.

A Day Away

Mid-August
and with the heat
the slow start of Monday.

Away finally.
Concrete and city open
into a wondrous summer day.

Sun   sky
green overgrowth wild enough
to repossess the road.

The beads beside me a kind of
flute   horn   string   anything
to join the flourish.

Monday :   Joyful Mysteries
Annunciation   Christmas
not confined   defined by some date.

The random grace of
an hour or day like this.

A Visitation
larger than the sweet sad tale
of unwelcome inn
makeshift manger and shed.

The full embrace for such descents
this skyscape   unbounded universe
unveiled now as only in summer.

An early Epiphany.

8

Inclusion as a Form of Gratitude

In Memoriam: Gerard Manley Hopkins
The Centenary of His Death – 1989

A hundred years away most now with me most mornings
You fetch me from bed more than lifelong sermons

From my first ever eastward window
I sense now through slats first glows
Rouse myself   even rise eager   see whether
Your *brown brink eastward springs*
Lovelier than yesterday
For years unfelt without your phrase I
Feel now first *the dearest freshness deep down*
I put on morning   attend tasks
Put on *patience, hard thing!* alas! this
Daily dress daylong falls often off
Yet part of patience is *piecemeal peace* to
Take tosses   fall seventimes   give
Self the selfsame mercy given

As far once as the Grand Canyon
I remember dawn   looking eastward
As tourists do
(without the questions of my cleft youth   and yours!)
          The wear of eons here...
          Were beauty or color here before our eyes?

In all of Aristotle no answer for me
Only years later yours:
          And what is Earth's eye, tongue, or heart else, where
          Else, but in dear and dogged man?

Now here my place more your Liverpool than Ribblesdale
And louched low grass all concrete this *the soil*
Is bare now, nor can foot feel, being shod.

Nonetheless.
Many mornings I tread soiled streets by
Shambled homes wanting as you Him hiding
For Christ plays in ten thousand places,
Lovely in limbs, and lovely in eyes not his
(how poorer my pen for distilling tears into diamonds).

Even here - and there - a flower
What if only weeds these pushing through refuse
And cement *long live the weeds* like
You I need beauty in all this havoc
Like you with words redeem *The Wreck*
Beauty will save us
Saved you   save me
Before I am undone

Midmorning
Amid rot at least relief upward
Cloud-puffball, torn tufts, tossed pillows
. . . heaven-roysterers, in gay gangs!

At walk's end a hospital and I about
Awful tasks over limp limbs
You, priest, ease where I with oil
Am priest where you were priest
And made sense of it:
this seeing the sick endears them to us, us too it endears.

Back now   about other tasks
Not able always to have you here
Always like dawn   the glow goes   you fade
Noon glare undoes often any softness
A *scaffold of score brittle bones*
I walk hours not all bad:
The poor press importunate and
All the others often enough annoying
Some joy: helping here   laughing there
A pleasant call, some sense of making it
Music even *keeps warm men's wits*

10

Sundown means Mass
Now Bread and Book and Cup nourish as you me earlier   now
Low-latched in leaf-light housel his too huge godhead.

Worst is the hour after dinner alone
When windows warm and families flock against
The black West   no mind
None are alone and all are rich for
Look at the stars!   look, look up at the skies!

Even back at noon first feeling fragile
About to come apart, I should learn your lead
Look up
Not of all my eyes see, wandering on the world
Is anything a milk to the mind so, so sighs deep
Poetry to it, as a tree whose boughs break in the sky.

Late now.   *Here! creep*
Wretch, under a comfort serves in a whirlwind: all
Life death does end and each day dies with sleep.
Mercy the quiet hours that are unconscious
Mercy more the morning with windows
to drink again *the brown brink*

Again *deep down freshness* to renew with
You I manage some sense *that we are wound*
With mercy round and round.

Writing

The press of this place.
How I understand Hopkins
catching the quietus
the sliver between penitents on either side
slide closing and not opening
until that elusive dangling word   caught
put down in darkness.
Verse a merciful distraction since
sin so dull at least in the listening.

Here the queue means doorbell
going off just as telephone goes on.
The importune poor smelling up the foyer
wanting plain bread or a can of beans
not forgiveness or grace or anything ethereal.

Save for a snatch or two there in Liverpool
even Hopkins could not catch
the coarse grain of frayed clothes.
Away to Ribblesdale for
the tail markings of a dragonfly.

Someone should catch this:
the tense set face of a grandmother
going again at children.

Here in that slip
between walk away and weary return
I stab at it:
smell   mood   frown   moment.

"One of his letters was written in the confessional while he was waiting for a penitent in an unusual break in the queue."

(*Gerard Manley Hopkins: A Very Private Life* by Robert Bernard Martin, 326).

13

Love Light

A ripe sun
failing from dawn to warm a winter day
reddens with anger   flattens
breaks in a thousand windows
like slack from a failing fire.

An incendiary evening
ends as orange softens into amber
in light-laced snow-snug houses set
in trees now ink lines on rice paper.

Christmas is such a softening.
Bible tales of floods and fires
give way to a human scene
with the warmth of a body huddle.

The Old Masters knew what they were about
with the light coming off the Child.

Madonna

Already weary of the store windows
I notice an old woman
framed in my windshield
for the moment of a traffic light
at a dark November corner
in a surge of early shoppers.
She is no shopper.
Her unseasonal white shoes   her transit pass
her worn daily bag are clues
on which I build her story
much as we build Bethlehem around
some words that fire the imagination.

As close as the end of my arm
I am as distant from her cold wait
as the comfort of a warm car
where the stereo gives the Christmas songs
"concert hall quality."

I imagine her going home now
from a day of laundry and late dishes
to needs open-mouthed and unattended.
A grandson, say, with some desperate story
needing her few new dollars.

The light changes and
I move deeper into winter
a Madonna disappearing
in my rear view mirror.

Requiem for a Sister

Old and quiet   she seemed lonely
far from love   (by human measure)

Elegant even in illness   after years of
she could look lovely in   nothing but starch
plain lay dress   black serge

Some secret   must have hummed in her
              pressed her gently
        for years beyond accustomed usefulness.

The daily trolley ride   (she was not alone)
              the school for problem boys
          the menial tasks of schedules, typing
                (*omnia fiant in caritate*)

Wire glasses   must have pressed
on raw wounds   the facial cancer.

              Hard for her to believe
          we wanted to embrace her.

For her funeral   the inevitable guitars
an honest effort   (the songs cannot say it).

          For me an added sadness:
      friendship offered and unexplored.

Postcommunion   renewing vows
her sisters' custom   (language starched overstated)

Despite the words   take home the sheet
in hope   promises so fruitful in her
              can make something
                  of me.

Hospital

ash wednesday should be omitted here
ash enough   the soiled streets
the limp limbs of this old woman
whom i tend with sacraments and such

                    too intent to notice
another woman cleaning closeby
so slight her presence she hardly sees herself
(gospel grace of left hand not knowing what right is doing)

i (scarcely) see her elsewhere also:
on elevators, say, almost hidden
no, humble   the poor mindful of their place

when easter comes with readings of
his appearing through closed doors even
eating to show his substantial self
i shall imagine him graceful as
the cleaning woman

Spring

"April is the cruelest month" indeed
melting winter into soiled sluices
like the bleeding veins of a city
lying wounded in the glare of surgery

The still cold sun
peels back the thin blanket
undressing corner lots suffering
nakedness as poorly as
our aging selves

Longer days almost unwelcome here
warming into summer
firing row homes into furnaces
forcing overwrought young bodies
        into crowded streets,
wanting night
even trouble as some relief
        of restlessness

Almost unwelcome
the new light stirs joy in children
schoolyard clatter grows more frantic
old lots put on green to
ease the emptiness

Life breaks through unlikely places:
a weed in a snatch of soil
on the medial strip of an expressway
a blossom falling from the crevices
of a ruined wall.

26

27

Holy Thursday: Mandatum

The pity of Monsignor Mitchell weary
waiting half a life for the terse
Roman rite to open up
on his knees   towel in hand
in an almost empty church.

No nonsigns   no nonsense with Mitchell
no gowned groomed matching men
his dogged daily walks   a gospel net
catching the sundry fish that
crowd now around the altar.

The full moon has Easter late in April
a warm night sends shoppers everywhere
street sounds pour through open windows
drowning the sound of water running
ewer to basin over bare feet

flooding into Mitchell   worn and uneasy
knowing that even his exhausted service
is unworthy of such immense signs.

Never rising from that knee-walk
his later years   a long Good Friday.

His Easter only now.

Good Friday: Adoration of the Cross

After my own obeisance
I find again the sedile
knowing from past years
the site and slant are perfect
for watching the procession of

arthritic old women half
grasping half holding on
hands knarled as wood knots
this kiss a rare showing
of patience that year round is habit.
Habitus: an old and learned word for grace.

Stumbling children are pushed forward
mothers without men touch warm
lips to raw wood   the one
embrace they know these lean years.
Gospel widows at the temple box
all their affection is outgoing
this gesture their two pence.

Last the addict daily at the door
here tonight because the lights are on
and this line must go somewhere.
Halfway up he sees me and
his new devotion will intend
the two dollars he will later want.

No matter.
Together we stumble to Easter
the *carpe diem* of the good thief
was, it seems, acceptable:
"Today you are with me in paradise."

Holy Saturday: the Great Vigil

Winter returns with dusk as
a raw wind chills our lean huddle.
Streetlamps and blazing downtown towers
eclipse my going on about New Light.

Yet belief is ever a lean grasp:
"We see poorly as in a dark mirror."
This night a shade of fiercer times
of Patrick on Slane with his fire
roaring into the full Paschal moon.

Or farther back
believers arriving as now
yet waiting all night
since word was He rose with dawn.

My hand as shaky as the small flame
I talk loudly to counter doubt
drown out street noise
move toward faith.

However frail these signs
here on schoolyard asphalt
we announce Easter.
Faith under siege can be hope.

Another kind of waiting.

Easter

Early Thomas Merton made us all
alter ego monks   eager visitors
heavy-eyed at vigils
singing in morning with Trappists
behind Psalters so huge that
page turning was a two-man job.

Sometimes someone went the distance
leaping from guest loft to choir cowl
a daring diver disappearing into white water.

One such
Charles (later Matthew) Kelty
Boston-born Irish at first a foreign missioner
a familiar Celtic saga
Merton lured him later on.

Loving the sound of his own voice
as much as any   (more!)
Kelty let words go
("Elected silence sing to me," says Hopkins)
slipped away into Kentucky woods
marking the seasons   years
turning great leaves of plainchant.

Not altogether quiet
now and then a note   a new homily
a peace walk to Washington
protesting Vietnam.

Easter 1990:

A Paschal parcel from Kelty
one word unadorned on
two folios fetched from some monastic cellar
as away alas as Latin
as forgotten as his farming praying self.

A spread sheet   an Easter feast
alleluia
over and over and over.
What relief from the many words
with which I gild this Easter!

Easter 1991:

Alleluia seems as lost as Latin
Quomodo cantibimus canticum Domini in terra aliena?
how sing Easter in the wake of war?

Like Kelty last year
we rummage our ruins
like disciples at Emmaus
break Easter bread anyhow
search the shadows
await a late Rising.
Alleluia   anyhow.

In Memoriam: Franz Jäggerstätter

A neighbor out early saw him leaving
looking back that February morning
toward this farmhouse from the gravel path
framed now by this kitchen window.

A wife fifty years a widow welcomes us
lights the stove to warm her guests against
the evening chill of early summer.

A friend of *Burschen* years saw him farther on:
"Go with God, Franz," he called.
The answer back: "You'll see no more of me."
The blessing uncomprehending of
a life soon ending early. The judgment
in before the verdict: *Frommigheit*   excessive piety.

What with wife and three daughters
and his going off . . . upstairs the old woman
shows us the great marriage bed
brought here as her dowry.

A tandem the villagers say still:
Franz and Franziska   a marriage
making each twice strong not half weak
giving grace as a sacrament ought.
Opinion here is that she allowed him.
Her silence was his assurance.

With summer wife and pastor Karobath
went to see Franz in his Berlin jail.
He had delayed this face-to-face appeal
for fear of giving in.

"I did not want my husband to die,"
she still insists nor did Father Karobath
himself in *Bezirksverbot* for speaking out.

The waiting room looked on a prison yard
where a truck came with Franz in chains
pushed off into a soldiers' circle.
"Franz," she screamed from the window
and he looked wildly about.

With a visit less than twenty minutes
he managed somehow a chocolate for
each his daughters.   Later Franziska
wrote: "Heavy-hearted we had to leave each other."

Here at table in her daughter's house
beside her own old home become now a shrine
my fellow pilgrim presents a timid gift:
his print of Franz from photographs with
fear the likeness would not suit her.

No. The gift is welcome
bringing first silence then apology
for emotions still alive
smoothed daily by faith
soothing oil on deep wounds.

A half century now
these houses fields and hills
still an indifferent stage
mute behind such sorrow.

The Greeks knew the cycle:
grief joy courage cowardice.
Wheat and weed grow together
Branau and Linz   homes of Hitler and
Eichmann only kilometers away.

No. No sudden strength this.
More the wisdom of a gospel virgin
not caught with lamp unoiled   more
a way of life revealed in prison letters:
    "It would not be too much
    a hundred kilometers on foot
    to attend a single Mass."

An echo of easier earlier years
alone of men at daily Mass
Franz and Father Karobath
and the older village women.

Yet not always so.
The village remembers more the *lustig* years
of bars and brawls and motorcycle.
Then an absence so mysterious that
visits home were secret.

Rumor that he was away at
Steiermark   a miner making extra money
while old parents could still manage.

Or did women trouble bring new expense
the need for distance. . .
No matter. Trouble can be grace
trimming the lamp as well as anything.

Exile and return and marriage
were making the new man
and not an Aryan supreme.

Farmer rather   and sacristan
fingering beads and Bible in the fields.
At night Franz and Father Karobath
planned resistance to the *Anschluss.*

Some remember the new seriousness
how the sacristan would bolt the door
against those coming late to Mass.
The same Father Karobath who
for aging needing parents
persuaded Franz away from religious life
wanted some compromise with conscription.

A procession of priests and persuasion:
    pastor and replacement pastor
    prison chaplains at Linz and Berlin
    a Greek chorus going
            "You must be practical
            your wife and children. . ."

All warnings absorbed by the new Franz
looking at life with his gospel lamp.
Family was indeed in mind
the painful part of the decision:
    "All my dear ones. . .
    I would spare you but you know
    we must love God even more than family."

Enter local bishop.
Franz' stand even then
a stone rippling still waters.
Franz summoned or bishop sought
the Linz prelate saw him:
    "I reminded him of his greater charge
    in particular for his family."

Priests themselves were being conscripted
his court-appointed attorney asks:
    "How can you unlearned in theology
    rush to such conclusions?"

Franz answers with the exquisite
love that judges none but self:
    "They have not received the grace
        to see things otherwise."

A charity as earlier for an informer
reporting the sermons which had Karobath removed.
All the village shunned the man
except for Franz.

The prison months a lifetime.
Lamplight flickered in the storm
a whirlwind: faith doubt worry
    "My dear children
    when your mother reads these letters
    your father will be already dead.
    He would have loved to come to you again."

Here now in this house
blessed by his blood offering
hard to give his offering sense
by any human measure.

By such he made no difference.
Third Reich and Great War
not less nor more for his stand.
Austria prospers in the
'economic miracle' of modern Europe.

Franz and Thomas More another tandem.
Franz had more with wife willing.
More had more in public station
standing up to Caesar   knowing
the crime was recorded   would
with centuries curb the crown.

Endurance saw Franz no further
than being brought closer as
some are by grace and fate to
the nuptials sought at daily Mass.

Before the headsman   we glimpse
a wedding already begun
as Franz declines a chaplain's care:
    "I am completely bound in inner union
    any reading would only interrupt
    my communion. . ."

After Saint Radegund all Austria
looks different   down the Danube
by boat Linz to Vienna
I see more clearly   sadly
the rivertowns   notice
abiding   the onion-dome
churches of this almost Eastern Europe
high behind great cloister
walls sturdy as the rock cliffs.
Signs as clear as roadside shrines:
the heart of Catholic Austria.

Like the rushing river
fierce questions intrude:
Why was Franz so alone?   Where
the Church so woven into life?
The Benedictine blessing of ordinary
family   fields   and daily life?

Is strength weakness when
weakness needs strength?   Is
what blesses hearth and sanctions power
hindrance for an apocalypse?
Too slack a sail for the whirlwind?

Twenty years on with
the Nazi horror in full light
the bishop who once discouraged Franz
could still dismiss him as
      "thirsting for martyrdom. . .
      more to be admired than imitated."

Here in Vienna as night comes
the great *Votivkirche* darkens
fills with Brahms   Vivaldi. . .
suddenly a west window burns
a blaze unseen by all but
this pilgrim fresh from Saint Radegund:
Franz ripping a cloth swastika
Franziska farther down praying at his grave.

With dusk the window dies
the flame goes in   goes home with me.
Tomorrow by accident or grace
another will notice
light his lamp from Franz
tomorrow and tomorrow . . .

In Memoriam: Simone Weil

Simone Weil dead fifty years
keeps me coming here.
The bronze-kept sunburst-housed sacrament
the still sister praying still
away at the altar end
behind rood screen and cloister grill.

An awkward arrangement this
accoutrement of Versailles and Sun King.
The Reformers eager to end excess
went: "Back to the Bible."
No enclosure.   No Greek accretions.

Unless Plato and Pythagoras
are a happy marriage for
a fierce Hebrew desert faith
taking Bible beyond ethics.
θεωρια [1] needs no reason more than self.

From my distance
I join the sister sunbathing
being bronzed   a transubstantiation
beyond words or understanding.

---

1 θεωρια the Greek word for contemplation

"Prayer consists of attention."   Simone Weil, *Waiting for God.*

"All Greek civilization is a search for bridges to relate human misery and divine
perfection."   Simone Weil, *God in Plato.*

43

44

A Gloss on the Obituaries:
Graham Greene 1904–1991

The smell of the wet wool
of my rain-drenched winter coat
on a gray Dublin afternoon and
suddenly you appear only days from your dying
earth-lingering   heaven-haunted   double agent.[1]
Smell summons you
the sense you most connected with memory.

Your Stanboul Train now at full stop[2]
no more murky stations   midnight layovers.[3]
You the new Diogenes   some latter day Lot
searching out sideyards for grace hidden in undergrowth.
Greeneland.[4]   A promontory falling into parables.
Your whiskey priests and prostitutes[5] mirror
you The Man Within[6]   clutching desperate hope
in the absence of anything   everything else.

For you most faith a futile mask
failing for want of struggle
the holding on   the other side of doubt.[7]
Aquinas would approve
these three abide: faith   hope   love.
In the seeming absence of the others
your hope that hope will see you home.

The damp wool dries. The scent recedes.
Like a ghost you are gone
wherever dark delivers us.[8]
Left here we have your stories
spy-drops for our own intrigue
more awkward   less eloquent than your own.

1 "Be a double agent—and never let either of the two sides know your real name" (*Newsweek* 15 April 1991).
2 "...this indomitable man who had always been on the move—one day in Moscow, the next in London or Panama" (*Irish Times* 4 April 1991).
3 "The great novelty of escape, betrayal, failure and guilt spent his life on the run from an abiding dislike of himself" (*Irish Times* 4 April 1991).
4 "Greeneland, the metaphysical landscape of his novels, was full of bad Catholics in various degrees of sin and doubt mostly repulsive" (*London Times* 6 April 1991).
5 "The basic element I admire in Christianity is its sense of moral failure... that is its very foundation" (*Commonweal* 3 May 1991).
6 "For experience of a whole century he was the man within" (*Irish Times* 4 April 1991).
7 "In a curious way I've always believed that doubt was a more important thing for human beings. It's human to doubt" (*London Tablet* 23 September 1989).
8 "Has our man in Antibes found revelation or darkness? (*Irish Times* 4 April 1991).

Sandymount

The black wash of Dublin bay
and in the wet sand a sign:
    Whoever wanders two hundred metres here
    risks fierce incoming tides.

James Joyce walked here   risked tides
went away on eagle's wings.
I cautious   stay safe
walk carefully
return at last to the familiar.

Kept man of the domestic church
secure   I seek further
the comfort of these surroundings:
chapel   sacrament   books
roadmaps for my rough within.

My steps are measured
never beyond easy return.
Hope hinged on the promise
that timid sparrows
are as watched as eagles.

Inishowen Head

This rise falls away to water
bringing the morning   green
and sun so bright on sea
that earth and sky are one.

Clouds
now reveal   now conceal
the glory going on.

This panorama opens me
floods in
now catches   now covers
I falter   fall into a shadow self
quiver like the blowing grasses.

Sheep stand where last night left them
lambs nurse   gulls feed
on the brown furrows of
a potato field plowed yesterday.

A nervous self drinks this hour.
The shadows surface
reassured by the larger landscape.

I shall stand here
warm my hands on this first coffee.

Let Inishowen in.

Retreat Hospitality
(for Loman, O.F.M.)

A turf plaque in tourist shops reads
in Irish:
   No hearth like one's own.

Yet times are
     when self is far from a warm place
Kavanagh's torturous road
       not near any end.

More the Irish monk forever abroad.
Exile as expression of the human condition:
   "We have here no lasting city."

Only wayside inns
a good Samaritan for our wounds
warm as the whiskey he offers.

His ear this attentive hour
a soothing service   a footwash so heeding
    that who serves   is served
    is hardly obvious.

Friendship as fine   refined
As the balance either side an apothecary scale.

Oratory: Easter Friday

The evening sun
overcomes a gray Dublin day
splashing through lace curtains here
onto the far white wall
brightness beyond any trace of the embroidery

This plain room
adorned now for Easter with
flowers   a large hand-lettered antiphonal
open to an alleluia
a white linen shroud
over an ordinary pyx
falls askew enough to distract me

The shroud too small
has one side short

Making the most of my distraction
I note we are a week from Good Friday
and the wound
that opening will be my access

Traffic Light

Wary of the contrariwise traffic
which has me looking the wrong way
only now up against me   the compact car
holding husband wife and child

An Irish face his   very like my own
once removed from this island where
I return now for deeper sense of self
some light on these later years

Your man made the commonsense choice
these Irish beds are cold at night
this Ireland no more self-sure now
than any other place

His constellation close at hand
a course as clear as the angels beside him
my fortune   fate   other Irish
wandering lonely monks
translating ordinary unrest into travel
peregrinatio pro Christo

Different for them   faith as well
endless   abundant as the oceans
carrying their tar boats wherever
providence   destiny   always a surprise

As much a stranger to their confidence
as to the warm huddle of the compact car
I motion them on   move on myself
more unsure than ever

50

France: *Inflight*

Casual airflight reading:
Einstein with affection naming
God "the Old One" but saying
the Mystery   a person is "absurd"

next from the flightbag a book
arriving by mail as I was leaving:
deLubac on the Church in Vichey France
a wound needing recovery

old deLubac was honest with
his report to Maritain telling
how French Catholics failed the Jews
during the Occupation

the Polish Jew beside me reminds
me (a priest) how "most killing
has roots in religion."   I
am back and forth
now Jew   now book   with

deLubac weaving that web
where I am lifelong caught
the Church. This mess from
apostles and early fathers opening
out into this awful century
of prelates caught in little
more than ceremony

even then though words from popes:
"Spiritually we are all Semites"
or deLubac: "the sweep of the Church"

these things snare me.   Against
all Einstein and my own despair
the hope   no, more the sense
that the Church   a gift
given us by a kind of incarnation
has still hidden the grace
I saw before disillusion

faith stirring that gift in me
as much as in deLubac in
me because of deLubac and others
my longlost saints never lost

despite the damper of my Jewish neighbor
something is unfolding in me as
I turn the pages of the book.

Paris: *Église Saint-Séverin*

Nostalgia or stubborn hope
whatever... the need to find this
grotesque near perfect Romanesque-
going-Gothic stone twist with
stained glass *flamboyant*
near *Notre Dame*   finally

half a century since priests here
took on an indifferent France as
though with psalms and tired faith-signs
grace could renew the earth

the thin Gelineaus and *La Nouvelle Théologie*
able at least to cross an ocean steal
into seminary reading rooms
nourish us eager for ordination

now diminished hopes or none at all
the new as humdrum as the old
more unseemly without a Latin veil

after streets changing names
Place Saint-Julien-Le-Pauvre become *Rue Saint-Séverin*
I am again revived by psalms:

    Consécration des Vièrges
en la fête de la Visitation de la Vièrge Marie
Bernadette, Brigitte, Marie, Michèle et Odile
sont heureuses de vous inviter...

Not many   not young as before
this old place still at it
faith overcoming world.

Paris: *Église d'Auteuil*

Evening Mass of the Ascension.
with the indifference of her eldest daughter
I expect an almost empty church
instead a full catch pours through
doors opening wide as nets into *Place d'Auteuil*

an older priest defers to cantor
a psalm of ascent "when from our exile"
followed by the last of Easter alleluias
inviting our ascension with an apse
mural of a pantocrator Christ
faded as my schoolboy French
unable even for the *Notre Père*

Masslong my ascent is hindered
earthbound by womanbeauty beside me
a division like faith itself wanting
us to live in two worlds at once

with communion she brushes by
her fragrance still another stay
yet the Feast says the flesh goes with us
I am glad she is here
her grace graces psalms
grace upon grace
everything is gift

Greece: *Cape Sunion*
Temple of Poseidon

Every windlap of water is
a bronze Brancusi fish
the sun multiplied a million
times across the Aegean

where my sight falls from
amber columns of a roofless
temple to sea below
lovelier than the azure sky
which makes the aquamarine.
My excited eye is back and forth:
now sea   now sky

These ruins ruin me   drain
what faith I cup in earthen-
ware   worn as these stones
          vacant now centuries

Better no myths. Expect
nothing but cerulean sky making
turquoise sea.   Yet hope
persists. Every downglance
starts the upward eyedance
now down   now up
"the heavens tell the glory of God"

Munich: *Frauenplatz*

A bronze gong of an afternoon sun hangs between the
twin towers of *Frauendom*
a dozen trees splash lacelike
shadows on water running
down Belgian blocks drowning
cast metal water lilies.

No one thing happening:
workmen descend the towers
in an outside construction lift
to make their way home.

A young couple near the water
have an eye for one another
another on their children
stepping lilypad to lilypad.
Others pass through oblivious
on their way somewhere else.

No one thing going on:
a landscape like the painting at the
Alte Pinakotek: "Platz Mit Eine Kirke"
by Jan van der Heuden.   Nothing
but sky   trees and an old church
unless the artist seeing and
catching this makes meaning.

Later at the *Neue Pinakotek*
I notice a "waterlilies" by Monet
and know that bronze fountain and
painting are all of a piece.

New Mexico

This desert morning unfolds
the possibilities of emptiness

onto lip and brim of blue dome
an all-around orange gathers
road dust   birdsong   mountains

into iridescence as magnificent
as *Sant' Apollinare* in Ravenna
where alabaster windows cast
amber into dark vaulted spaces.

Seeping thus inside
the morning touches
places   scars   seldom warmed.

Something more of self
and early answers.

The song which awakens
travels barren distance
for meaning more than human hearing.

Teilhard might call it
"excentration"
the invitation out of self
to a glory now beginning.

No longer
need that fearful self near burst
for effort to enclose a universe
in such a fragile dwelling.

Bavaria: *Ettal Monastery*

A mix of plainchant and incense
rises into a rococo vault
of cherubs   emperors and unicorns
with relief that the monks mind
the music more than ceiling.

Alleluia *moderato* even on Pentecost.
The economy of the long haul.
Andante   moving more within.
Night of the Senses.   The best prayer
is not to know one is praying.

City Church

Archeological almost
the awe   then the ascent
through doors shut since Sunday
tight as Pharoah's tomb.

Within
sunlight pours down on darkness
seeps through stained glass
tells the old stories to no one all week
sweetness spent on empty air.

The irony of these old places
as away as unimportant now as Bethlehem
lost in the projects of the poor
who need the beauty more than bread.